GOD INCOGNITO

augsburg publishing house, minneapolis

GOD INCOGNITO

by roy a. harrisville | *a series of lenten sermons on the passion according to st. john*

GOD INCOGNITO
Copyright 1956, Augsburg Publishing House
Library of Congress Catalog Card No. 56-7248

Printed and manufactured in the United States of America
by Augsburg Publishing House, Minneapolis 15, Minnesota

DEDICATION

*To my son and daughter whose cries
only occasionally interrupted the
delivery of these sermons.*

ACKNOWLEDGMENTS

The author wishes to express his gratitude to the following publishing houses for permission to quote from their publications:

The American-Scandinavian Foundation: *Philosophical Fragments,* by Søren Kierkegaard.

Harper and Brothers: *Death Be Not Proud,* by John Gunther.

Pearn, Pollinger and Higham, Ltd., *The Man Born to Be King,* by Dorothy L. Sayers, and *Bevis,* by Richard Jefferies.

Radio Corporation of America and Mr. Robert Shaw, *The St. John Passion,* English translation by Mr. Shaw.

Sheed and Ward, Inc., *The New Testament,* A New Translation by Msgr. Ronald A. Knox.

*"Theologus crucis . . . est de deo
crucifixo et abscondito loquens . . . ."*

(Martin Luther, W. A., I, 613. 23)

None of the rulers of this world could read
His secret, or they would not have crucified Him
to whom all glory belongs.

(I Corinthians 2:8)

CONTENTS

"He, as soon as he received the morsel, had gone out; and now it was night"

(John 13:30, from a translation of the New Testament by Ronald Knox).

"Lord, Thou our Master, Thou whose Name in
     ev'ry land is glorious (and ever glori-
     fied shall be):
Show us by this Thy Passion Hour,
That Thou, the very Son of God,
     At every time,
     Yea, in the hour of deepest woe,
Wert ever glorified."

(From "The Passion According to St. John" by Johann Sebastian Bach, transl. Robert Shaw).

 *a double cross?*

IN DANTE'S inferno, the last circle of hell contains the souls of those who have betrayed their masters. In the center of it stands Satan, stuck fast in the ice, visible only from the waist and up. He has three faces, and under each face a wing by which he struggles to raise himself out of the frozen hell, but which only fans a breeze and freezes him more firmly to the spot. He is weeping with all six eyes; down his three chins tears and bloody foam are gushing. In each mouth he chews a sinner with his teeth. For the middle victim, the biting of those jaws is nothing compared with the tearing, for at times his back is completely stripped of skin. "That soul up there, which suffers greatest punishments," says Dante's guide,

1

"is Judas Iscariot, he who has his head within, and outside plies his legs."

In response to such a description, most of us would say that the dirty double-crosser got what was coming to him, that he belonged in the last circle of hell just where Dante put him, along with Brutus and Benedict Arnold and the "dirty little coward that shot Mr. Howard." For somehow our conviction that Judas deserves a worse hell than the next man is coupled with the idea that the One whom he betrayed was only a helpless, passive victim of his treachery. On the one hand, the meek and lowly Jesus, the gentle, indiscriminately loving Jesus, who seemed never to take a hand in His own destiny, and on the other, the conniving, scheming Judas who lived with Him, possibly even shared a passionate devotion to His cause, and then sold Him down the river, while He Himself looked on, either helpless to do anything about it, or not wanting to, because of some hope that Judas would reconsider. And on the face of it the Bible gives the impression that the story of Judas and his role in the Christ-drama introduces a foreign, alien element, that Judas was the X-factor, the unknown quantity which could not be reckoned on. What the Gospel writers say of him reflects a certain horror and embarrassment at the thought that this man should have been the cause for things getting out of hand, that this man—a disciple!—should have seized the bit between his teeth and run away with things. Reading this part of the life of Christ, one feels moved to great sympathy for Jesus, the Underdog, who passively waits while Judas plots. One wishes he could have been there to warn Him about Judas, as though He didn't dream He had hugged a scorpion to His breast when He called Him to be a disciple.

Children have many strange dreams. One which I remember best from childhood is a dream of Jesus and the twelve at the Last Supper. Aside from all the incongruities of that dream—I was wearing a civil defense helmet, and the scene itself took place on the stage of my high school—I recall how desperately terrified and frustrated I was by the fact that I knew Jesus was about to be betrayed but didn't know it, and that I was powerless to help Him. I was held prisoner. But I was near enough to yell and be heard, and had one arm free enough to point a finger. "Judas!" I yelled, and then awoke. Aside from whatever "clinical" implications such a dream may have, in the dream Jesus played the role of a passive victim, a role most of us have assigned to Him in this affair of the betrayal.

It is pretty much agreed that Judas Iscariot perpetrated the double-cross to end all double crosses. And yet, there is more here than meets the eye. There is something hidden here, hidden beneath the seeming victimization, beneath the

3

apparent passivity, something else obscured by Judas' awful presumption, but it is here, all the same. Whatever it is, it was there long before the crucifixion. It was there at the high-water mark of His career, when the crowds began to desert Him and in answer to Peter's oath of loyalty He said: "Have not I chosen all twelve of you? And one of you is a devil." So He knew what Judas was about, even then! But what is stranger and perhaps more fantastic is that He deliberately chose Judas one of the twelve in the full consciousness of what he was intending! Why did He choose him? Was the choice made in a moment of forgetfulness, or was what the Gospel writer assumes to be Jesus' knowledge of His betrayal really only an intuition which He decided to disregard?

On the day of his betrayal, Caesar had an intuition of his death—that is, his wife Calpurnia did, and Caesar gave in to it, ostensibly to humor his wife. But undoubtedly he had misgivings of his own, for he first consented to remain away from the senate on that fateful day. But when he considered the possibility of his looking the fool should that intuition prove groundless, he turned with an air of dash and bravado, and like the typical Adam blaming Eve he said: "How foolish do your fears seem now, Calpurnia! I am ashamed I did yield to them.—Give me my robe, for I will go. . . ."

Caesar's intuition was illogical, it was ground-less—unless you interpret the soothsayer's warning "beware the Ides of March!" as furnishing his fear with a reason—but Christ's was no intuition. He knew who would betray Him, and still He chose Judas!

That hidden something crops up again in the story of Mary and her anointing of the feet of Jesus. Judas objected to the "waste," because, as the story goes, "he was a thief; he kept the common purse, and took what was put into it." But if Jesus knew, why was the man left with the bag? Was it a weakness in Jesus, an inability to face up to the reality that one of His own was a traitor? Such an explanation doesn't harmonize with what we know about Jesus. He was a realist. But mightn't it be possible that in this one instance, where one of His own disciples was involved, He lacked the capacity for admitting the awful truth? If I were to furnish you proof that someone close and dear to you, someone you love greatly, were false, wouldn't your first reaction be to disbelieve? For a moment, at least, wouldn't you be incapable of facing the reality of such a falsehood? You would be, that is, if your love for that person were something of long standing, as Jesus' love for Judas was. That incapacity for facing up to the reality of the treachery of someone close has figured in a thousand tragedies, in real life and out of it. It is that incapacity which makes so poignant and bitter that scene near the statue of Pompei where Caesar, recognizing his beloved Brutus to be one of his assassins, cries out: *"Et tu, Brute? then fall, Caesar!"*

Whatever it is that is concealed beneath the obvious and the apparent, it was there at the Last Supper. Jesus and the twelve had gathered in the upper room for their last meal together. Having seated themselves and having begun to eat, Jesus immediately revealed that He was about to be betrayed. The disciples were thrown into confusion. They began to ask: "Lord, is it I, is it I?" Judas was there; he asked the same question, and he got a reply: "Thy own lips have said it," but in the din and confusion no one but Judas himself heard Christ answer his question in the affirmative. Later in the conversation, too late for its being regarded as having any connection with the idea of betrayal, Jesus said to Judas: "Be quick on thy errand." Why didn't Jesus expose him? Why did He permit the others to harbor the notion that those words spoken to Judas were an order to buy groceries for themselves, or food for the poor? For, as the evangelist says: "None of those who sat there could understand the drift of what He said." And more: Judas knew now that Christ knew what he intended to do. Ordinarily, that would have meant that the jig was up. But Judas didn't cancel his plans; he didn't postpone his little rendezvous with the mob in the garden. Why didn't he? Was it that he believed he could count on Jesus to keep their secret?

Finally, that hidden something is there when those two, Jesus and Judas, met face to face in the garden, when from the lips of Jesus came those cryptic words recorded in Matthew: "My friend, on what errand hast thou come?" Had He forgotten what had taken place only a few hours before in the upper room? Or had He chosen not to remember? What kind of question is this from One who only a moment ago was anticipating betrayal, who knew beyond the shadow of doubt who it was who should carry out the deed?

Somehow, whatever reasons we have given thus far for Jesus' attitude toward Judas don't seem to be the real ones. We feel instinctively that to regard them so is to paint a picture completely out of harmony with Jesus as we know Him. For fundamentally, the net result of accepting those reasons would be to admit that Jesus was a suicide, nothing more; that, like Socrates, He had the possibility of escaping death—for He knew who would betray Him and could have averted betrayal—but for some strange reason, possibly because of great disappointment and despair at not being believed, or, like Socrates, in obedience to some transcendent law of reason, He chose to die. But this is an impossible admission. The reason which seems closest to the truth is that Jesus chose Judas, not for the same purpose as He chose the others, but for another purpose—for betrayal; that in the full and complete knowledge that Judas was a thief He left the unhappy man to an inner "ripening of soul," entirely aware of the consequences; that He deliberately and purposely kept the betrayal a secret between Himself and Judas because He had determined that this was the way He must die; and, finally, that He put that strange question to Judas in the garden to encourage His enemies in their belief that they were taking Him by surprise, and so nerved them, emboldened them for His arrest. In other words, in Jesus, the omnipotent God was assuming the dominant role—even in His betrayal—a role hidden, veiled and obscured by the willful treachery and initiative of Judas. To be sure, we hear of Judas acting, Judas plotting, Judas bargaining and Judas betraying, and that is what confuses us. For it appears that Judas is in control here, and indeed, Judas himself thinks and believes he is in control. But that seeming passivity, that apparent weakness of Jesus, that apparent inability to part company with Judas is only His incognito, His alias, by which He disguises His sovereignty. That "hidden something" is the truth that Jesus Himself is really in command! The tables are turned! It is the Christ of God, not Judas, who is in the driver's seat. That doesn't mean that Judas is a pawn, that he does what he does against his will.

God never violates human personality. Judas is heart and soul after those thirty pieces of silver, all right, but he becomes an instrument in the hands of a God who veils His power and His strength beneath shame and indignity and silence. Was it a double-cross? Undoubtedly it was for Judas—"I have sinned . . . in betraying the blood of an innocent man"—but it was not for Christ, not for the God who conceals His majesty so profoundly that what appears to us and to the world to be weakness, indecision and passivity is really only strength and power and might incognito!

"There, then, Judas came, accompanied by the guard, and officers sent by the chief priests and Pharisees, with lanterns and torches and weapons. So Jesus, knowing well what was to befall Him, went out to meet them; Who is it, He asked, you are looking for? Jesus of Nazareth, they answered; and He told them, I am Jesus of Nazareth. And there was Judas, His betrayer, standing in their company. When He said to them, I am Jesus of Nazareth, they all shrank back, and fell to the ground. So, once more, Jesus asked them, Who is it you are looking for? and when they said, Jesus of Nazareth, He answered, I have told you already that I am Jesus. If I am the man you are looking for, let these others go free. Thus He would make good the words He had spoken to them, I have not lost any of those whom Thou hast entrusted to me. Then Simon Peter, who had a sword, drew it, and struck the high priest's servant, cutting off his right ear; Malchus was the name of the servant. Whereupon Jesus said to Peter, Put thy sword back into its sheath. Am I not to drink that cup which my Father Himself has appointed for me? And now the guard, with their captain, and the Jewish officers arrested Jesus and pinioned Him"

(John 18:3-12)

"O boundless love, O love beyond all telling—
Wherefore Thou made this street of tears Thy
    dwelling!
I live within the world, its pleasures cherish,
And Thou must perish!"

stealing the show

ONCE in a blue moon, walking down old Broadway, you will see some old fellow changing names on a theatre marquee. The show hasn't changed; it's the same. He's taking down the name of the star or the prima donna and replacing it with another, a name no one knew yesterday, the name of some newcomer or ingenue who stole the show, made the star and the whole company appear to be only the supporting cast, when in reality they were intended to carry the lead. I have heard it said that whenever John Barrymore appeared on the stage, no one dared predict the outcome. Once he set foot on the boards, careful programming went out the window. When comedy was required, he would soliloquize, something from *Hamlet,* or *Julius Caesar,* or *Richard the Third.* He could always be counted on to steal the show. This characteristic no doubt endeared him to his audience, but perhaps to no one else. There is nothing quite so crushing for an artist as losing his spotlight to another. Perhaps you remember, a year or two ago Milton Berle lost his to a guest, and he has never quite recovered.

That night in Gethsemane, the mob was the star again, the self-confident, arrogant, bloodthirsty mob. It had always been the star, it had always had top billing. The scenes had changed now and then; some of the cast kept appearing and disappearing and reappearing again, but it was always the same show and the same star: "And *they* said to Him," or *"they* tried to trick Him in His speech," or *"they* took Him to the brow of the hill and tried to throw Him over," or *"they* bargained for thirty pieces of silver." It was always the mob, always the mob doing this or that, the mob saying this or that. When we begin the reading of the New Testament, the mob appears to have the stellar role. We continue, and there is no change in billing. We read further, and it is still the mob; further yet, and just when we think Jesus is about to take the spotlight and give the drama a new twist, it's the mob again.

It was the mob again that night too. The scene with Jesus and His disciples gathered for supper in the upper room was only a kind of interlude, an intermezzo, time to let the cast get ready for the big, dramatic climax. Indeed, it seems as though everything Jesus ever did was only an interlude, a chance to let the star change and get ready for the next act. In Gethsemane He would play His part, but "they" had determined it should be only a minor role. The attention of the audience really belonged to the soldiers, to the officers from the chief priests and Pharisees, to the torches and lanterns, the swords and the staves. The scene this time was an arrest, with the mob in command again. The whole drama had been building up to this. This was to be the scene where the star strutted his stuff, where the hero triumphed. There were to be brilliant speeches ("Aha, we've got you now, you villain!") and gestures, a clanking of chains and lanterns and flickering lights, perhaps even a few blows struck, with Jesus and the others cringing in terror and slapping their foreheads as all good villains do when they know the game is up.

But, as Bobby Burns has it, "the best laid plans of mice and men gang aft agley." The mob swarmed into the garden with lights and weapons and a voice in the darkness cried: "Who is it you are looking for?" (Do you remember that passage in Bach's *Passion* in which the Christ booms out those words in a rugged bass?) The mob answered, and then came the words which shifted the focus, words like roaring thunder and pounding surf, words which reached back to Abraham and Isaac and Jacob, to Midian and to Sinai, reached beyond all that to the beginning of man, and beyond that, too, to creation itself, and, even beyond that—reached back to nothing but blinding majesty and omnipotence and awful purity, to God Himself: "I am He!" "And they all shrank back, and fell to the ground." This wasn't the way the thing was supposed to come off. The mob didn't play the part we would assume it should play if it really had the lead. The Bit-player had stolen the show.

Well, such may happen, and still things may go on as rehearsed. The star may pick up the pieces, pretend nothing has happened and still carry on to a brilliant finale. At the Metropolitan a celebrated diva, in the middle of an aria which required her lifting up a jewel case, discovered to her complete befuddlement that a practical joker had loaded it with stones. The audience roared with laughter as the star stood there, grasping and sweating, holding the thing as though it were an iron girder. She lost her audience, but quickly regained composure and continued singing. Jesus had stolen the show, but it was only for a moment—things really turned out in the end as they had been planned. He lapsed back again into the role of the passive victim, the helpless, hopeless Jesus in the clutches of the aggressive mob. He was arrested in the end. For a minute there, He was the Jesus we have always wanted Him to be, but He finally submitted.

Or did He? Is there something we may have forgotten about Him which makes questionable whether what took place in Gethsemane was really an arrest? Something which makes us doubt whether the "play" really went off as planned? You remember, early in His ministry, on the last great day of the feast He stood up in the street to cry "If any man is thirsty, let him come to me, and drink!" They wanted to seize Him then and there; they even called out the militia to fetch Him, but, as the story continues, "No one laid hands on Him." Another day He stood up in the temple and He said: "Believe me, before ever Abraham came to be, I am." They took up stones to kill Him then, and again, so the story goes, "He hid Himself, and went out of the temple." When He revisited His home town Nazareth, and declared that Isaiah's prophecy of the Servant of God had been fulfilled in His own person, His neighbors said, "Is not this the son of Joseph?" and they dragged Him out of the synagogue to a high hill and would have thrown Him down head first, "but He passed through the midst of them, and so went on His way."

Couldn't He have escaped this time also? They hadn't recognized Him in the garden; they would never have known who He was if He had not first asked the question, "Who is it you are looking for?" and then revealed Himself. He could have gone scampering off into the woods with the others, and at worst could have lost His shirt in a struggle to get free, just like that anonymous young fellow in the story of Mark. And a bit later, after clumsy Peter hacked off someone's ear in the melee, didn't He make it clear that escape was His but for the asking—to use the words of Matthew: "Dost thou doubt that if I call upon my Father, even now, He will send more than twelve legions of angels to my side?" Was there involved here only a temporary embarrassment of the mob, only a sudden shift of focus and then a just as sudden return to the business at hand? Or had the Bit-player affected the plot too; had He changed the drama from a well-calculated, well-timed arrest into something else?

We are obliged not only to change the names of the "leads" here, but also the name of the play, indeed, the drama itself. At Gethsemane the mob was no longer in command. Jesus was. What happened at Gethsemane was not an arrest at all—it was a surrender. The apparent, seeming, supposed arrest in the garden; the apparent, seeming, supposed aggressiveness of the mob was only His incognito by which He chose to hide His complete command of the situation. The shouts and the yelling, the lanterns and the shining helmets were only the veil to disguise what really happened there. And if you should ask, "How can you be so sure?" I would answer by telling you to begin at the beginning and discover for yourself that it is Jesus who really takes the initiative in arousing the opposition of the crowds. True enough, the mob plots and plans, the mob devises, the mob lies in wait, and sometimes it really does appear as though the mob is the only actor in this divine drama. But who speaks first and awakens the reaction of the mob, though He speaks ever so quietly and softly? Who gradually and carefully intensifies the anger and hatred of the mob, brings it to a boiling point, first with His claim that He knows what God is about, then with His miracles by which He demonstrates that He is sent by God, then with His words of His own closeness to God, and finally with His claim that He is one with God? It is Jesus! Who is it who whets their appetite for His arrest, brings it finally to a ravenous hunger for blood and death by His repeated escapes from their attempts to trip Him up in His speech, to build up a case against Him, by His repeatedly eluding their attempts on His life? It is Jesus, intent on death, death for the life of the world, raising the anger of His opponents to a white heat, that that death for your life, my life, might be a foregone conclusion.

And on the eve of His betrayal it was Jesus who hated and despised the sword and taught men the love of God who deliberately permitted His disciples to carry two weapons on a feast day—a felony—in order that He might be numbered with the transgressors in His death, just as the prophet had said! His declaration "I am He," meant that He sought no secrecy, no hiding-place. His death was a free offering, and the hour of His death was of His own choosing, God's own choosing! Those words of Jesus to the mob concerning the twelve —"If I am the man you are looking for, let these others go free"—these are the words of a Person who has assumed the role of command, the words of a Person from whom no one on the earth can take that which belongs to Him. Until now He had removed Himself from those ordered to arrest Him. But now the hour had arrived, and He surrendered Himself. To the mob He said, "Your hour has come now, and darkness has its will," but it was really still His hour, for it couldn't have become their hour if it had not first been His, if He had not given it to them, made them a loan of it. Beneath His incognito, beneath the veil and disguise of His submissiveness and helplessness, He was still in command, and the mob knew it. Because He had stolen the show, changed the plot, made a fiasco of their arrest, they would kill Him now, but not with satisfaction, not with glee, perhaps not even out of revenge, but only out of despair and madness, out of guilt—they would kill Him out of guilt, and, paradoxically enough, because they had to. The Son of Man had to suffer by their hands. It was a case of Gulliver's submitting to the Lilliputians, willing to be bound by an absurd, little people whom He could have crushed in a moment, for the chance to see what lay ahead, for what the writer of the Hebrews called "the joy that was set before Him." So the mob had never really been the star. The eye of the audience had really always belonged to Jesus, God incognito!

"Take Him yourselves, said Pilate, and crucify Him; I cannot find any fault in Him."

(John 19:6)

"The bondage, Lord, which Thou didst own
    From this our freedom riseth;
Thy dungeon is our mercy throne,
    And liberty abideth.
Didst Thou not choose a slave to be,
We all were slaves eternally."

who's on trial here?

WHEN you and I hear of a man's being indicted for some crime, our sympathies usually lie with the prosecution. Picking up our newspapers and reading the crime of which a man is charged, we tend to pass sentence upon him with such remarks as "the rotten fellow ought to get the chair," or, "I hope he gets what's coming to him," meaning that he deserves the worst. Perhaps the reason for our sympathies lying with the prosecution and seldom with the accused is to be found in our tendency to believe the worst of a man. The carefulness with which juries are picked, the lengths to which the court will go to insure that each member on the panel has formed no previous opinion or judgment is an attempt to counteract that tendency in us to believe the worst, to sentence a man without fair trial. Though the principle is stated the other way around, and justly so, for all practical purposes, with us human beings a man is guilty until he is proven innocent.

The trial of Jesus, however, is an exception. Our sympathies in this case lie with the Accused. In His case, that "higher," "nobler" sense in us, that "sense of justice and fair play" has been aroused, and we feel pity for that lonesome Man, arraigned before the gigantic machinery of the state in the person of Pontius Pilate. In the British courts, the indictments always read: "Rex *versus* John Jones"—the King, the Crown, *versus* John Jones—and one gets the feeling that it is a case of the whole empire against one man. It was the same on that long night over a thousand years ago. Rome, and everything that word calls to mind, against one lone Man, Jesus Christ. But sometimes Rome could be surprisingly sympathetic, and so Pilate gave Jesus an opportunity to plead His case. Just as anyone who reads about this trial feels instinctively moved to pity for Jesus, helpless against the might of Rome, so must Pilate have felt. It was a golden opportunity for Jesus. But what is so surprising and disappointing is that He did not seize the opportunity. He just stood there, dumb, silent, like a guilty man!

A few hundred years before, another great man stood trial, charged with corrupting the youth of Athens, with teaching men not to receive the gods Athens worshipped, with introducing new and strange gods. But when he appeared before the court of his accusers, he took advantage of this situation. Indeed, he took charge of it, for he cross-examined his prosecutor and confounded him with his sophistry and irony. Though he claimed it was immaterial to him whether he lived or died, he did make sure that his name and character were cleared of false charges; he did make sure that the world forever after would regard his executors as the biggest fools on earth for putting to death such a wise and virtuous man; he did say that his death would be of great disadvantage to his city. Perhaps you have heard somewhere those ironic words of Socrates in his defense: " . . . if you kill me you will not easily find another like me, who, if I may use such a ludicrous figure of speech, am a sort of gadfly, given to the state by the god; and the state is like a great and noble steed who is tardy in his motions owing to his very size, and requires to be stirred into life. I am that gadfly which god has given the state, and all day long and in all places am always fastening upon you, arousing and persuading and reproaching you. And as you will not easily find another like me, I would advise you to spare me." Jesus could have pleaded His case. Or, at least, if He were indifferent to His fate, He could have shown His accusers up to be the fools they really were, as Socrates did. But He didn't. And yet, He was on trial for His life!

But was He? There must be a case, a brief against a man before He can be tried. There was none against Jesus. A man must be indicted for something before He can begin to plead His case. There was no indictment against Jesus, and so no case to plead. Oh, the people brought those nonsensical accusations against Him, but they weren't worth a fig to Pilate. He never cared about those little squabbles, the hair-splitting and the haggling over religious technicalities which always went on in Jerusalem. In fact, he had such contempt for the Jews' religious scruples that on one occasion he plastered their town with the Emperor's images, and only removed them because he was reluctant to wipe out a whole town, when the whole town raised a fuss.

In another century other Pilates would burn and crucify "heretics," but it was this Pilate's job to condemn only political enemies, and not even the wildest stretch of the imagination could make this meek Jesus out to be a political risk. It would have been terribly unjust—Pilate, Tiberius, Rome, mighty Rome, sentencing this harmless Person to death on the testimony of these nervous, excitable fuss-budgets, who were themselves sworn and avowed enemies of Rome!

A tragicomic scene, the kind of scene to re-
mind us of Hugo's *Hunchback of Notre Dame,* in
which poor, one-eyed Quasimodo, the bell-ringer,
the king of fools, was flogged unjustly and to the
amusement of the filthy rabble; his deformed,
misshapen hulk stripped of skin, and Quasimodo,
the kind, gentle, stupid Quasimodo, grunting and
spitting under it all. So, three times, while scurrying in and scurrying out of his "chambers," now
prattling with the mob, now questioning the Accused, Pilate cried: "I cannot find any fault in
Him!" Under the circumstances, you would expect such a case to be thrown out of court for lack
of evidence; you'd expect the judge to bang his
gavel and growl, "Next case!" Or, perhaps, you'd
expect him to let the poor Fellow off with a slight
reprimand, and then turn Him over to the custody
of His parents, if He had any, with the suggestion
that He consult a psychiatrist. But he didn't;
Pilate didn't let Jesus go. Why didn't he? Because
he couldn't—he just couldn't!

Someone hearing this account of Jesus before
Pilate for the first time might be tempted to yell,
"Do you call this a trial!" Even those who have
heard it a thousand times might be moved to ask,
"Is it really a trial?" Yes it is. *Someone* is being
indicted here; judgment is being rendered against
someone, no matter how frightfully things are going. There really is a trial here. But it is not Jesus
who is on trial—it only appears so, it only seems

so. Then, who is on trial? Pilate, Pontius Pilate. To be sure, the position of the two men throws us off base for a moment: Pilate in the seat of judgment surrounded by the standards and eagles of Rome, and Christ standing in silence before him like a common criminal. We are confused for a moment, but in the next we know that what we see there is only an optical illusion. We feel instinctively, we sense immediately when we read the account of this event, that Pilate's occupying the judge's chair has nothing whatever to do with his *real* position, his *real* situation; that whatever he may appear to be, he is not really the judge but the judged, and that the case against him is clear and unequivocal. Pilate is the defendant, Pilate, bound to act according to strict law, bound to maintain order, to protect the law, to decide upon right and wrong, but who does not, who renounces the very thing he is bound to do, surrenders the clear law; Pilate, who "from fear of the Jews" lets himself be determined by "political considerations" like any petty politician, in order to stay in office. Pilate, who rewards the wicked—sets Barabbas free!—and punishes the good. Pilate, who can't condemn Jesus because He finds Him not guilty, but who surrenders Him nonetheless, and in surrendering Him surrenders himself, disgraces the state, makes it a den of robbers, an irresponsible clique. Pilate, who like all small men with small minds, humiliated at having to give way to those whom he hates, revenges himself on them by calling Christ their King and refuses to change the mocking inscription on His cross.

It is Pilate who is on trial here, but not only Pilate. The whole world is on trial, the whole world of men and history and nations and people who can do nothing else to Jesus Christ but make Him suffer and die! . . . The world, for whom Pilate is nothing but the mouthpiece; the world which can only kill the innocent and let the guilty go free; the world which lies under judgment and so must make room for another kind of world where men will live without fear of the Pilates or the Caesars.

All the outward circumstances of the trial—the incriminating silence of Jesus and the apparent power of Pilate; his "Dost thou not know that I have power to crucify thee, and power to release thee?"—are only an optical illusion, the incognito by which the Son of God conceals the truth that He stands in judgment over Pilate. The seeming loneliness and solitariness of Jesus up against the majesty of Rome is only the veil to hide the power and the majesty of the Great Judge who shall some day come to judge both "the quick and the dead," though in this moment that veil seems heaviest, thickest, darkest.

And, Pilate was sentenced. Can anyone doubt that he was sentenced, sentenced to what has been called a "hateful immortality," when on every tongue, in every land, in every generation, in every week of the year these words find their way to Christian lips: "Suffered under Pontius Pilate," *"Passus sub Pontio Pilato," "Leiden unter Pontius Pilatus," "Il a souffert sous Ponce Pilate"*? The gifted English essayist, Dorothy Sayers, has written a brilliant radio drama called *The Man Born to Be King,* in which she interprets the dream of Pilate's wife which moved her to beg her husband to let Jesus go free. In the play Pilate asks: "Claudia, Claudia, tell me—what was this dream of yours?" Claudia answers: "I was in a ship at sea, voyaging among the islands of the Aegean. At first the weather seemed calm and sunny—but presently, the sky darkened—and the sea began to toss with the wind. Then, out of the east, there came a cry, strange and piercing, and I said to the captain, 'What do they cry?' And he answered, 'Great Pan is dead.' And I asked him, 'How can God die?' And he answered, 'Don't you remember? They crucified Him. He suffered under Pontius Pilate.' Then all the people in the ship turned their faces to me and said: 'Pontius Pilate'; in all tongues and all voices; even the little children with their mothers—your name, husband, your name continually—'he suffered under Pontius Pilate!' "* So it *was* Pilate, and not Jesus, who was on trial!

*From *The Man Born to Be King,* copyright 1943 by Dorothy L. Sayers.

"So Jesus went out, carrying His own cross, to the place named after a skull; its Hebrew name is Golgotha. There they crucified Him, and with Him two others, one on each side with Jesus in the midst."

(John 19:17-18)

"My dearest Saviour, wilt Thou answer:
Since Thou this hour the cross hath taken,
    And since Thou sayest: It is fulfilled!
    Am I from death forever freed?
Am I, since Thou in woe hast ended,
To heaven's realm commended?
    Is all the world redeemed this day?
Thou canst for pain indeed not answer,
Yet bowest Thou Thy head to say, in silence:
    Yea, yea!

    Jesus, Thou who knewest death,
        Livest now forever.
    When I yield my dying breath,
        Vain is my endeavor
    If to Thee it is not turned,
        O my dearest Master!
    My redemption Thou hast earned
        By Thine own disaster."

 *the gibbet*
the victor's car

WHEN I was a boy, my parents took me to see Cecil B. De Mille's screen-play on the life of Jesus called "The King of Kings." During the crucifixion scene, I sobbed so loudly an usher threatened to order us out of the theatre.

On the face of it, that is the kind of emotional reaction to this scene one would expect—pity, sobbing pity for Jesus, the innocent Victim, helplessly nailed to a cross, His body displayed in full view of every profane eye, a hideous burlesque. Apparently the crucifixion of Jesus was only a pathetic martyrdom, tragic and unexplained, and the cross on which He hung only the supreme unveiling of human injustice. We wish He could have come down from that cross—"Save Thyself, and come down!"—but He didn't come down; He hung there, helpless, pitiful, putting the period to a great career with that shameful death.

He made great claims, He did great things, but His death made it appear that all those claims and all those things were nothing more than the claims and deeds of any other ordinary man. We are asked to believe in this Man, to look beyond His death to something else which can vindicate those claims and those deeds, but our reason tells us death is so terribly final, that it is questionable whether there is anything to be seen beyond it. There is no historical evidence, no archaeological evidence anywhere to prove that something else happened to Jesus after His death. His crucifixion is the great question mark drawn over Him. We would like to believe He was what He said He was, but that death prevents us, it makes agnostics of us, makes us pause and say, "How can we be sure?" His death forces us to the conclusion that though He was the greatest of them all, though human life does indeed become more meaningful when it is lived as He lived it, nevertheless His life story ended in martyrdom, just as the life stories of so many other great and noble men. His crucifixion gives plausibility to the idea that the last chapters of those books we call the Gospels are the works of later hands in later times, times when people wished to believe more of this Man than they had a right to believe; that those accounts of a rising from the dead were legends once needed to give men courage for life and comfort in death, but that we do not need them now because we may face life and death realistically.

Whatever it may mean to face the fact of Jesus' crucifixion realistically, that realism is not without its tinge of sadness. Richard Jefferies, the author of that English classic on boyhood, *Bevis, the Story of a Boy,* describes his hero's reaction to a portrait of Jesus in death. "The crucifixion hurt his feelings very much; the cruel nails; the unfeeling spear; he looked at the picture a long time and then turned the page saying, If God had been there, he would not have let them do it!" If God had been there! But apparently He was not—apparently the death of Jesus was only a martyrdom. We imagine that if Jesus really were God, there would have been another ending to the story, the kind of ending we would expect of a God.

And yet, aren't we forced to admit that God doesn't always do what is expected, that He very often reveals Himself in a manner precisely opposite to that which a man would normally and naturally expect? By and large, isn't the God of the Bible a Person who always seems to act contrary to our idea of Him? And, even apart from the Bible, we all encounter situations and circumstances in our lives which continually shatter our ideas of God as we imagine Him to be. That's the story of religion, men discovering, generation after generation, that ideas of God which were held in the past, those little systems, won't hold water any longer because of things which have happened since, because of things which men in the past didn't take into account, perhaps because they didn't know about them.

If there is a God, then He is continually shattering our notions about Him. For if He were not, we wouldn't have all those bitter, disappointed people in the world who doubt God, hate God, because He has turned out to be an entirely different kind of God than the God they imagined Him to be. Any man who believes in God has "trouble" with Him, because God always violates our idea of Him, He always shatters the neat little systems we have constructed about Him, He seems never to be able to be pigeon-holed. Just when we think we have Him in the palm of our hand, He escapes our grasp, somehow, sometime. Again and again where God is concerned, we are compelled to stand in awe of Him and cry with the apostle: "Who hath known the mind of the Lord? or who hath been His counsellor?" So, mightn't it be true in the case of Jesus' death that here too God is not acting according to plan, that is, our plan? Mightn't it be that our expectations, our assumptions, our presuppositions regarding what a God ought to do once He gets into the kind

34

of situation Jesus got Himself into can't really apply to Him, since He almost always goes contrary to our expectations? Mightn't it be that in this case too, God has somehow managed to slip from our grasp? For if as the Gospel writers have said, Jesus knew about the cross all along, and yet on the eve of His death cried out: "Father, the hour is come: glorify Thy Son, that Thy Son also may glorify Thee!" then mightn't that be a clue that Jesus regarded His death as something quite different than we have regarded it—as a glorification, a victory, and not a martyr's death at all? That intense preoccupation with His cross from the very beginning of His life, that talk of "laying down life and taking it up again," that conscious, deliberate, and from our point of view, almost suicidal surrendering of Himself to death might be the clue that what appears to us to be a pathetic martyrdom is really something else!

It is something else! The passion of Jesus Christ is not a "passion" but an action, not a defeat but a triumph! What we see there on the cross, the nails, the cruel thorns, the broken body, are only the veil, the covering, the mask, to hide the One who is really there. Hanging on the cross there is the Victor-God who conceals His identity in the suffering, defeated Jesus. The veil is thick—indeed, here it is thickest of all, because man, the world, naturally associates victory with power and strength and conquering might and not with weakness and humiliation. For how can egocentric, self-seeking, self-asserting and proud man understand that the way of humiliation, the way of suffering and self-sacrificing love was the way in which the Almighty God would fight and prevail? It never occurs to man that God might act otherwise than he would act if he were God. It never occurs to him that what he expects of God, God almost never does. But there, where the world sees the exact opposite of victory—only defeat and tragedy and pathetic martyrdom—there Jesus triumphs. Strange as it may appear, this cross is the proof of the power of God, for it is God and only God who has the power to reveal Himself in such a way that that very power itself is hidden and cannot be seen! Richard Jefferies' Bevis cried, "If only God had been there!" He was there! Beneath that veil of the suffering Jesus who gave Himself away, there hid the King who rules, beneath the covering of that weak and helpless Christ who sacrificed Himself and offered Himself there was the Victor who asserts Himself, manifests His power and might. What beautiful dramatic, unbelievable irony! The Almighty God, so hidden, so veiled, that men could spit upon Him, crucify Him, kill Him, believing Him to be someone else; His incognito so impenetrable that all the devils in hell could launch their attack upon Him—and yet, in the midst of all, as a Man being and remaining God, defeating man at his own game, triumphing over hell on its own home ground!

Why did He do it? Why did He veil Himself? The answer to that question can only be given in the form of another question. How should we have known the glory of God in the face of Jesus, how should we have been able to come to that God, to look into the face of that God, but through the weakness in which He was crucified? This veil, this incognito is not a cheap trick, a thing unworthy of God. The only way in which He could reveal His fatherly nearness, His pleading, His mercy and His grace was to become a Man like other men, a Man able to suffer and die, like other men.

One of the most beautiful analogies to this deity veiled in humanity ever written is Søren Kierkegaard's, contained in his *Philosophical Fragments*. A king once loved a humble maiden. But he was troubled by the thought that after their marriage she might never forget what he wished to forget—that he was a king, and she only a humble maiden. If this memory were to waken in her soul, what would become of their love? In that case, the maiden were happier to remain in obscurity, loved by an equal, content in her little cottage. But, though the maid might be content to be a nobody, it would not satisfy the king, because he loved her! How should he solve the problem? He *could* so intoxicate her with joy that she would forget who she was in the joy of what she had become. But that would be a deception, even if the maid did not know enough to feel deceived. Or, he could show himself to the maiden in all his pomp, and make her forget what she was in a worshipful distraction. This might also satisfy the maiden, but not the king, who desired her glorification and not his own! There was only one way, to become the maiden's equal, to appear in the likeness of the humblest man, and to say to her: "Do you now really love me?" This way would be dangerous. The maid could refuse him then; he would have to suffer the bitter agony of an unrequited love then, but any other way would involve a deception. And right here is the explanation for God's becoming flesh. He donned the habit of the "humblest man." Here is the explanation for His being crucified, for dying. He endured the pain and agony of an unrequited love. Any other way would have been a deception. To return to the analogy, the gloomy Dane writes that if the king had revealed himself to the maiden as her king, she would have loved him only because he was the king. This would have made him weep and say: "To think that you could prove so faithless, and so wound my love! Is it then only the omnipotent wonder-worker that you love, and not him who humbled himself to become your equal?"

Precisely because God veiled Himself in the suffering Christ, His revelation was not a deception. The way in which He appears to us on His cross is the only possible way in which we can love Him without being forced to it, without an ulterior motive. But once loving Him, it is possible to understand that He really is the King after all, that the gibbet, the cross, has become the Victor's car, the Conqueror's chariot. It is possible to believe that those nails are His sword and shield, those thorns a Victor's wreath, that broken, bloody body His shining armor. He reigns, He conquers, He triumphs from this tree!

"After this Joseph of Arimathea, who was a disciple of Jesus, but in secret, for fear of the Jews, asked Pilate to let him take away the body of Jesus. Pilate gave him leave; so he came and took Jesus' body away; and with him was Nicodemus, the same who made his first visit to Jesus by night; he brought with him a mixture of myrrh and aloes, of about a hundred pounds' weight. They took Jesus' body, then, and wrapped it in winding-cloths with the spices; that is how the Jews prepare a body for burial. In the same quarter where He was crucified there was a garden, with a new tomb in it, one in which no man had ever yet been buried. Here, since the tomb was close at hand, they laid Jesus, because of the Jewish feast on the morrow."

(John 19:38-42)

"Rest well, Thou holy body sleeping,
That I no longer rue Thee, weeping,
    Rest well, and let me too, rest well.
The grave that is prepared for Thee,
And holds no further grief for me,
    Doth open Heaven wide,
    And close the gates of Hell.
Ah, Lord, Thy dear sweet angels send
In my last hour, my soul attend,
    To Abraham's arms bear it.
This body, in its narrow room,
So softly rests from pain and gloom,
    And waits the day prepared it.
Ah, then from death awaken me;
Unbind my eyes that I may see
In boundless joy Thy Holy Face,
My Saviour, and my Throne of Grace!
Lord Jesus Christ, oh hear Thou me,
I will Thee praise eternally!"

the last laugh

JOSEPH KLAUSNER, the Jewish scholar, has written a story of the life of Jesus for Jewish readers. Immediately upon relating the events of Jesus' death and burial, he adds the words: "Here ends the life of Jesus, and here begins the history of Christianity." What the celebrated professor means by these words is that the death of Jesus is the point at which historical fact ends and fiction begins. Whatever is said of Jesus following His death depends no longer on observable, scientific proof, but on such things as visions and dreams and hallucinations.

And indeed, whenever we read the account of Jesus' death and burial, the mood which prevailed with those who loved Him and saw Him die is somehow transferred to us: the mood which allowed that there was nothing left to do but to bury Jesus and remember Him. So there followed that same sad, meaningless activity connected with His burial which plagues every one of us whenever we bury our own dead—Joseph of Arimathea begging the body from Pilate; Pilate relinquishing it; Nicodemus and his boxes and bottles of myrrh and aloes; the winding sheet; the sepulchre. While Jesus was on the cross they could still hope for a miracle; they could still weep for Him—while there is life there is hope!—but His death appeared to be the end, really the end. He had ceased to be a part of the present, or the future. He had become pure past, only a memory. Some day, some careless fellow would stumble on His grave, discover His bones and comment on the futility and irony of life.

Do you remember that scene in Shakespeare's Hamlet, in which the prince came across the skull of an old friend who had been court jester in his boyhood? "Alas, poor Yorick!—I knew him, Horatio: a fellow of infinite jest, of most excellent fancy: he hath borne me on his back a thousand times; and now, how abhorred in my imagination it is! my gorge rises at it. Here hung those lips that I have kissed I know not how oft. Where be your gibes now? your gambols? your songs? your flashes of merriment, that were wont to set the table on a roar?" Then Hamlet, musing on the irony of death, let his imagination run riot and trace the corruption of the Greek hero Alexander, from his death to his turning into a handful of clay used to plug a hole in a beer-barrel : "To what base uses we may return, Horatio! Why may not imagination trace the noble dust of Alexander till he find it stopping a bung-hole? . . . Alexander died, Alexander was buried, Alexander returneth into dust; the dust is earth; of earth we make loam; and why of that loam whereto he was converted might they not stop a beer-barrel? Imperious Caesar, dead and turn'd to clay, Might stop a hole to keep the wind away: O, that that earth which kept the world in awe Should patch a wall t'expel the winter's flaw!"

To all intents and purposes, Jesus of Nazareth would go the way of Yorick, or Alexander, His handful of clay used to plug a hole, or His skull a reminder to some later generation to cry: "Alas, poor Jesus!" It appears as though His enemies were having the last laugh. During His lifetime, they had been made fools of, had stung and suffered under the lash of His tongue, but now He was dead, and the stupid ones huddled together and quaffed their wine in a toast to their victory, and the halls were filled with laughter and music and dancing. And the bright ones planned how they could set to rights all the damage He had done. "Crucified, dead, and buried"—here is the point where belief and unbelief, where the saint and the sinner, where Ignatius and Augustine and Luther and Calvin join hands with Voltaire and Bob Ingersoll and Nikolai Lenin, the former piously and reverently, the latter matter-of-factly, but join hands nevertheless. For Jesus died, and He was buried. It really seemed to be the end. His enemy had the last laugh!

What was there left for those who loved Him to do? What is there left for us to do? Say that it is possible to overlook the fact of His death, the objective brutality of His burial, and to see in it all a release, a deliverance, or even a death for others? How does one overlook death—death is real, it is decisive. Or, should we say that His life was so pure and so wonderful that death couldn't obliterate it? That He was so great and the memory of Him so strong, that, like George Washington or Abraham Lincoln He will live forever in the hearts of His countrymen? Even memory comes to an end, sometime.

A few years ago, John Gunther, the American commentator and author, wrote the life story of his son Johnny who died of a rare and unusually fierce brain tumor at the age of seventeen. The story was called *Death Be Not Proud*. He described the unusual mental capacity of the boy— he had rare enough talent to correspond with Einstein—his love of life, his inconquerable spirit, his calmness and philosophical attitude in the midst of the agonizing tedium of operations and

44

x-rays and treatments. Commenting on Johnny's burial Gunther wrote: "All that is left of a life! There Johnny was, so pale, so slim and handsome, in the tweed suit with a spot on the lapel, he always had a spot on his lapel, and a bright striped necktie—with what valor he struggled to tie that necktie in the last hopeless weeks—here he lay placidly in the small chapel full of flowers, with his face sweet and composed and without a trace, not an iota, of struggle or pain, and we said goodbye to him, Frances and I and a clustering group of friends. We said goodbye. But to anybody who ever knew him, he is still alive. I do not mean merely that he lives in both of us or in the trees at Deerfield or in anything he touched truly, but that the influence, the impact, of a heroic personality continues to exert itself long after mortal bonds are snapped. Johnny transmits permanently something of what he was, since the fabric of the universe is continuous and eternal."

Is that all that can be said of Jesus? It is small comfort if you regard death as something real. In fact, it is a naive attempt to soften the reality of death, a childish refusal to face the fact that it is really the end, *if* it really *is* the end, and I imagine Gunther believed it was for Johnny. You can't worship a memory, believe in a memory, build a Church on a memory. And precisely what Gunther wrote of Johnny has been said too often of Jesus. But death for Jesus was real, terribly

45

real—it wasn't the sleep of a rosy-cheeked child who can be awakened—death for Jesus was decisive, it really appeared to be the end. All those romantic, unrealistic and childishly naive sermons at Easter time about His influence and His impact and His heroic personality are small comfort if Jesus' death was really the end. His death was real, and whatever there may be for us beyond it, death will be real for us too.

As real as that death was, as decisive and final as it seemed to be, a light fell there on that tomb—the light of the third day! That light didn't make the death any less real; it didn't justify any refusal to come to grips with death in all kinds of romantic talk about a spirit or an influence or an impact or a heroic personality, but it did make clear that the death of Jesus, which really seemed to be the end, was not the end at all! That light which shone made it possible to face Jesus' death, and our own deaths, realistically. It made totally unnecessary all that naivete we hear at funerals. Because though that death was real, it was not the end. The enemy had laughed prematurely.

That great light which shone on Easter day makes it clear that Jesus Christ, though His death seemed to be the end of everything, though His Godhead and His infinite power were so veiled in death that that Godhead and power were visible to no other eye but His own, nevertheless did not cease to be God! Even in death, Jesus had the last laugh! His enemies were powerless to overcome the deity hidden in the humanity. They were cheated of what seemed to be their choicest Victim, just when they thought they had Him most securely in their grasp. Even in death, Jesus Christ was in control: the myrrh and the aloes, the winding sheet, the sepulchre, were only the disguise under which He hid His might and His glory. That is what the writer of the book of Hebrews means when he writes: "And since these children have a common inheritance of flesh and blood, He too shared that inheritance with them. By His death He would depose the prince of death . . . !"

The death of Jesus was an activity, a destroying, a breaking up of death itself, and a glorious making alive. By dying, He took the sting out of death, broke it up in business, bankrupted it, robbed it of its reason for being a fearful, horrible thing, changed it from a punishment to a doorway to life. Read the New Testament and see that because of Jesus' death, death has ceased to be a punishment for guilt. Our guilt has been removed and so there is no need for punishment. Rather, it has become a necessary prelude to eternal life, since "flesh and blood cannot inherit the Kingdom of God."

It was not Jesus who lay in death's strong bands, but death bound captive by Jesus. Death, on its way now to the execution chamber, about to be annihilated just as the apostle says: "He will wipe away every tear from their eyes, and there will be no more death, or mourning, or cries of distress, no more sorrow; those old things have passed away." Under the disguise, under the incognito of a cold, lifeless body, my Redeemer was at work, destroying the very thing which first seemed to be destroying Him! While His enemies were thinking and believing they had done with Him, while they were yelling, "Here endeth the Gospel!" "Here endeth the life of Jesus!" He was having the last laugh!

Think what this means! Though I must face my death realistically—as something decisive—though its reality is something I can't avoid with all my romanticizing or philosophizing, nevertheless it is not the end for me! Because of that Easter light I am not at my wits' end to develop some Guntherish doctrine which can help me forget the barbaric cruelty of death. Death is death, but it is not the end! In Jesus, but only in Jesus, am I able to cry:

> "Death, be not proud, though some have called thee
> Mighty and dreadful, for thou art not so;
> For those whom thou think'st thou dost overthrow
> Die not, poor Death; nor yet canst thou kill me!"

". . . so much has been written down, that you may learn to believe Jesus is the Christ, the Son of God and so believing find life through his name."

(John 20:30-31)

"Take the wings of faith and fly now,
  (—Ah, where?) His cross draw nigh now,
  Your salvation blossoms there."

tearing off the mask

EACH one of us wears a mask. That is, the face we turn to other people and to the world is not usually the real one. Human life always involves a certain amount of play-acting, a certain amount of concealing what we really are behind a mask. One psychologist calls this mask our *persona,* the Roman actor's word for the mask worn on the stage. When two people meet for the first time, they usually do not reveal who they really are. They turn to each other their masks, pictures of themselves as they would wish to be, or as other people would wish them to be. But in normal relationships, if a warm friendship were to develop between those two people, you would see them gradually removing their masks and revealing to each other their true identity. (A person becomes abnormal when he can never get from behind his mask, when he identifies himself with his mask to such a degree that no one can penetrate to the true person beneath it.)

And yet, none of us ever fully reveals to another who he really is. Two friends, two companions, even a husband and a wife, may live together for years, each believing he knows the other as intimately as his own self, and then something will occur to convince them both that there are things, traits, characteristics, thoughts in them both which the other can never fully fathom or understand. We live our lives in intimate relation to one another, and yet, somehow, we never completely reveal our true identity. We are never able to tear off the mask, or, at least, to tear it off completely.

To a certain extent, the same is true of God. "To a certain extent," because any analogy we draw from human life and apply to the living God always breaks down somewhere. But it is by no means obvious, either to the physical eye or to reason, that Jesus Christ the crucified Man of Nazareth is the Incarnate Son of God. The veil, the mask which He wears, the mask of His suffering, dying humanity is so opaque, that it is impossible to prove by reason or argument or logic that the living God, the omnipotent God is the One who stands behind that veil. It is impossible to prove that Jesus is God because that God-ness of His is so screened from our sight. He is a Man just like other men. He thirsts, He hungers, He sits Himself down by a well to catch His breath. He wears dusty clothes and shoes with holes. He suffers, He dies. And it is this manhood, this flesh, this humanity of Jesus which makes His Godhead something impossible to be seen with the eye, or to be proved.

This often troubles us, and we cry to Jesus with His disciples, "Show your hand, Jesus! Tell them who you are! Tear off your mask, come out from behind your veil!" But instead, He always meets us clothed in the garment of a creature, in a vesture belonging to this world. There is nothing about Him which is suitable to disclose that He is God. If He is the revelation of the Almighty God, then that revelation is not an unveiling, but a veiling. And the veil is thick!

It has been said that the moment a person puts on a mask, he changes into another being temporarily, that in a certain sense his whole body changes appearance and proportion. If that is true of ordinary human beings, it is much truer of Jesus, for His humanity is not just a covering or mask which everyone knows is a mask and which can be quickly taken off. It is not a kind of swallowing up of what He really is by what He seems to be. *He is really a Man,* a Man who suffered and died, and that is what makes it so impossible to prove that He is God. It is not at all apparent that when Judas betrays Him, it is He who is calling the turns; not at all obvious that when He is arrested, He is stealing the show; not clear that He is not on trial before Pilate but Pilate before Him, nor that His death is not defeat but triumph. How then can we be so sure that what we have said about Jesus up till now is really the truth about Him? How can we be sure that He *is* God, exercising His majesty and power in this humiliation and death, when He appears to us to be so utterly human and nothing else?

We know, we are sure, because we believe. The majesty and power of God in Jesus is something which can be seen by faith, but only by faith. The hopelessness and helplessness of the suffering Jesus is only a mask or veil to hide His true identity, His Godhead—but that can never be demonstrated by reason, only by faith. Again, let us return to the analogy taken from human life. There are times when you have an intuition that the side someone is turning to you is not the only one. You feel that he is something else, something more than he seems to be. You don't know why you feel as you do—there is no reasonable explanation for that feeling—and yet, you know, he is something else than the mask he wears makes him out to be. You and I very often use those little saws such as "Still waters run deep," or "There's more than meets the eye," to describe people who impress us as being something else, something more than they appear to be. It is faith which sees that "something else," that "something more" in Jesus. As obtuse and as dull as the people were, as His disciples were, they followed Him because they saw in Him something more than He seemed to be. And it was their faith, however childish, superstitious, however fragile and weak it may have been, which made them see Him as He truly is.

This faith by which we see Jesus for what He is is not a human thing. It is so tiresome to hear those oft-repeated statements about faith's beginning where the brain leaves off, about our not being required to reason things out but only to believe. As though faith were the enemy of reason! As though faith were a crutch to help us along when reason gets tired and can't move another step, or a wet-nurse for reason until it can hobble around on its own feet.

Faith is not a human thing, but as long as men regard it as a human thing they will keep right on calling it an enemy of reason, or a crutch, or a wet-nurse. It is none of these things! It is different, different because it belongs to God, and reason belongs to the earth. When Simon Peter at Caesarea Philippi turned to Jesus and said "Thou art the Christ, the Son of the living God," Jesus answered, "It is not flesh and blood [human reason, human desire], it is my Father in heaven that has revealed this to thee." It is faith which tears off the mask, faith which seeks God and finds Him there in Jesus, finds Him concealed most profoundly in that Babe who sucks at the breasts of Mary, in that Man who hangs upon the cross. Even then, the answer to the question, "Who is Jesus?" is not completely solved, because faith is still faith and not sight. The mask is not entirely torn away. Some mystery still remains. The glass which mirrors God does not disclose all that might conceivably be learned about Him; even what it does disclose passes understanding. In one sense, even to believers that God who is in Christ remains unfathomable.

That is what makes faith such a great dare, such a bold, rash leap into the dark when everyone else thinks and believes there is nothing but a big hole, an abyss there! Faith means to believe in the power and the majesty and the omnipotence of God working in the weakness and pitifulness of Jesus; indeed! *in spite* of that weakness and pitifulness. Faith means to see with the eye of God, to see Him at work where others see foolishness and superstition and lunacy. Faith tears off the mask! Faith says with the gloomy Dane: "Behold, where he stands—God! Where? There; do you not see him? He is God; and yet he has not a resting-place for his head, and he dares not lean on any man lest he cause him to be offended. He is God; and yet he picks his steps more carefully than if angels guided them, not to prevent his foot from stumbling against a stone, but lest he trample human beings in the dust, in that they are offended in him. He is God; and yet his eye surveys mankind with anxious care, for the tender shoots of an individual life may be crushed as easily as a blade of grass. How wonderful a life, all sorrow and all love: to apprehend the danger that all men may be destroyed, and yet only so to be able really to save a single soul; his own life filled with sorrow, while each hour of the day is taken up with the troubles of the learner who confides in him! This is God as he stands upon the earth, like unto the humblest by the power of his omnipotent love. He knows that the learner is in Error—what if he should misunderstand, and droop, and lose his confidence! To sustain the heavens and the earth by the fiat of his omnipotent word, so that if this word were withdrawn for the fraction of a second the universe would be plunged into chaos—how light a task compared with bearing the burden that mankind may take offense, when one has been constrained by love to become its Savior!"

Dear reader, I am anxious that you tear off that mask. But it can only be done by faith, not by that reflex action inherited from pious parents, or by that mere assent to propositions which some people call faith. Faith which tears off the mask, tears away the veil of the Man Jesus, the suffering, helpless Victim, and sees the Deity there, the Godhead, the power and the glory and the majesty, is something which embraces a man's whole being! How can anyone suppose that anything less than faith, anything less than giving oneself completely captive to Him can make him see in that Jesus more than a poor, helpless Victim of circumstance, and Christianity more than an unbelievably expensive monument to the memory of a mere man!

There is no way to tear off that mask, to see Jesus for what He truly is, without that leap in the dark we call faith. Until you can make that leap, take the hand stretched out to you in the dark—just as a child in a darkened room takes the hand of his mother, trusting her to lead him safely to the light—you will never see Jesus. You will see only a man, a victim, a John Brown or an Abe Lincoln, but never Jesus. Without faith He is always, eternally, merely what He seems to be. But if you are one of those curious, childlike ones, if you have ever wondered who God is and what He has done, believe what those who loved Him said of Him, and you will see soon enough for yourself! And some day, even that in Jesus which still remains a mystery to faith will cease to be a mystery, "For we know that when He comes we shall be like Him; we shall see Him, then, as He is." Faith tears off the mask!

*"Next day, a great multitude of those who
had come up for the feast, hearing that Jesus
was coming into Jerusalem, took palm branches
with them and went out to meet Him, crying
aloud, Hosanna, blessed is He who comes in the
name of the Lord, blessed is the king of Israel.
And Jesus took an ass' foal, and mounted on it;
so it is written, Do not be afraid, daughter of
Sion; behold, thy king is coming to thee, riding
on an ass' colt. The disciples did not understand all this at the time; only after Jesus had
attained His glory did they remember what they
had done, and how it fulfilled the words written
of Him."*

(John 12:12-16)

*"BENEDICTUS QUI VENIT IN NOMINE
DOMINI!"*

 *the hidden king*

O<small>N A CLEAR,</small> fresh morning, a long time ago, when the winter rains were finally over, and the first grass began poking its way through the sodden, stony earth, a wave of humanity from the south swept up and over the ridge where the Mount of Olives begins its ascent, where a man could see the summit of Zion, rising, terrace upon terrace from the palace of the ancient kings, with its castle and frowning towers and magnificent gardens. The wave descended a bit, and the white, gleaming towers withdrew behind the intervening ridge, but all of a sudden it swept over another ridge and reached a level of smooth rock, and in an instant the whole city, separated from Olivet on the east by the valley of the Kidron, and on

the west by that of Hinnom burst into view, looking for all the world as though rising out of some
deep abyss. And that wave broke and came together again about one Man, like a wave which
parts and meets again over some great rock, a
Man, riding, riding, riding, and as a flood which
leaves debris and flotsam in its wake, that wave
left palms and leaves and clothing, and when it
reached the ledge where the holy city lay beneath
it, it met another wave, a wave from the north,
and the two waves became a sea, and the sea sent
up a thunder and a roar: "Hosanna! Blessed is He
who comes in the name of the Lord! Blessed is the
King of Israel! Hosanna!"

Somehow, the story of that Palm Sunday long
ago has always seemed to us to be out of context,
set as it is in the midst of all that blood and
death which marks the Lenten season. Somehow
it appears as a kind of pause or *entr'acte,* a time to
catch our breath before striking out for the lonely
hill of Golgotha. We have felt that what happened that day was one time, at least, when Jesus
was acknowledged for what He truly was, one
time when He got what really belonged to Him.
They called Him a king. Apparently they knew
who He really was. We have even felt that Palm
Sunday gives us some kind of right to speculate
about the crowds, to suppose that they weren't
really responsible for Jesus' death after all—for
how can you cry "Hosanna!" one minute and

"Crucify!" the next?—to suppose that that responsibility must have lain elsewhere, on Pilate, perhaps, on the soldiers, or on Judas, but not on the crowds. They knew who He was.

Palm Sunday is not out of context. It is not a pause or an *entr'acte*. It is not a white shaft of light in the midst of the gloom. It belongs just where it is, for it is the high-water mark of man's unbelief. The crowds did not know who Jesus was. They called Him a king, and a King He was, but not their kind of king. His real kingship, His real lordship was hidden, veiled in a disguise. And the irony of it all was that the King of Kings and Lord of Lords, the One by whom the worlds were made, the Redeemer of the earth, was being trumpeted into town like any cheap, gaudy, conquering hero. The real royalty was hidden—the crowds never saw it. What Jesus really was was hidden deep beneath what He appeared to be, beneath what the crowds wanted Him to be.

We may speak so categorically because of two things: the silence of Jesus, and that miserable little animal on which He rode. What was Jesus doing all this time? Holding up His fingers in a "V," waving to the stenographers and office boys poking their heads through the office windows and throwing out the confetti? No, He was silent. He never said a word. And, He rode an ass. The kind of king they thought they were hailing belonged on a white charger, but He rode an ass on an errand of peace, not war, peace through suffering and blood and death. The crowds lost sight of the King in a king. So close they were to seeing Him for what He was, uttering from their lips the glory and the praise which really belonged to Him, and yet, not seeing Him at all, not praising Him at all, but someone else, someone they had dreamed up, a product of their own imagination.

And after it was all over, Jesus fled and threw Himself down on that lonely hill above Jerusalem and He sobbed: "Ah, if thou too couldst understand, above all in this day that is granted thee, the ways that can bring thee peace! *As it is, they are hidden from thy sight.*" They had missed the King. They couldn't get beneath the veil, beneath the covering to see who was really there. They took Him for what He seemed to be, just a candidate for public office.

It is the same with us. When Jesus comes, we do not see Him for what He is, the King; His royalty is hidden. It is hard for us to behold the King of Kings behind the disguise of a Man who pleads and begs with us to believe Him. When we encounter Him, wherever it may be—in the Bible, in the Church, in another Christian—it appears as though we are on the throne and He begging us for a boon, for our faith, our trust, our devotion. Look at Him there on every page of the Scripture, pleading with men, getting down on

His knees like a beggar before them, without any kind of pride, going anywhere and everywhere to win a disciple. Is this the way in which a king ought to behave? Because He doesn't act like a king, but rather like a beggar, men can't see the deity and the omnipotence and the lordship. Because His word, His kingly word, is not a command, but a heartfelt pleading, men can spurn it, reject it, disbelieve it. When He could plunge us into hell for not believing it! Because His Church, the Body in which He lives out His incarnate life, seems such a pitiful, abject thing, men may ridicule it. When He could threaten us all with death unless we find our life in it!

Ironic, isn't it, that He, the King, should meet man in this way, that He should never meet us as the One who demands, but always as the One who asks, never as the One who takes but only gives, gives Himself, appearing never in the robes of His Godhead, but always in the rags of a beggar, risking a beggar's fate? The King, the living God, riding on an ass! What irony!

But it is the irony of His love. For He will never frighten man, never overwhelm him. He has respect to the human personality. He wants man to be truly personal, truly himself, coming to Him, crowning Him, singing "Hosanna" to Him, but never because he must. It is nothing less than God's love which makes Him so jealous for our freedom that He will appear to us in such a way that we have the unbelievable power of saying "No!" to Him, the unbelievable power of confusing Him with someone else, of singing "Hosanna" to Him when in reality we are singing to someone else. It is nothing less than His love, His divine love which permits me to take up His word and read it without trembling, treat it as though it were any other ordinary word—Shakespeare's or Byron's or Keats'—nothing else but love which permits me to pray to Him as though He were my equal, without being struck down for all my presumption! Love which permits me to utter His name so casually, so absent-mindedly, so parrot-like, without fear of immediate reprisal.

But couldn't Jesus at least have spared Himself this one indignity? Couldn't He have refused to ride that day, to be mistaken for someone else? Or was it that He let Himself be swept away by that mass of shouting, sweating humanity because He thought for a moment the crowds would receive Him as the One He truly was? Was is that He decided to make this one concession to the twisted hopes and dreams of His disciples regarding an earthly king? No. He rode because a king must ride, even the King of love. He let them throw their palms and shout their hosannas because a king deserves palms and hosannas, even the King of love. Whether or not He would be mistaken for someone else, something else, He was still the King, and He must reign!

There is a moral or two hidden in this story. The first is that the love of God is so great and so selfless that it compels Him to make Himself a person of no reputation, to take on the form of a servant. And the other is that whether in the disguise of a servant or not, whether confused with someone else or not, whether properly identified or not, He must reign, He must put all His enemies beneath His feet, because He is the King! He doesn't ride like a king; He comes like a beggar, but He must come, because He is the King! He may appeal to you as though His life were not complete without you; His summons to you may appear more as a request, a beseeching, but He must summon you because He is the King! Hidden, veiled, covered by a humanity which can suffer such indignity, such buffoonery, stumbling through the royal arch of Jerusalem like Hugo's Quasimodo through the streets of Paris, a king of fools, but King nevertheless!

We must right that wrong done nineteen hundred years ago. We must compensate for the misunderstanding of those foolish crowds. Palm Sunday is not a pause or an intermezzo, a "breather" we take before plunging into the agony and gloom of death and crucifixion. It is celebrated to right a wrong! What the crowds did not see, we must see.

The covering, the veil beneath which they could not penetrate, we must penetrate. It belongs to us by faith in that humble riding King of peace to make amends and proclaim Him as the One He truly is! We must right the wrong, let the world know that what men believed to be only a petty king was really the Lord, to whom the kingdoms of this world belong, the Lord who shall reign forever and ever! That the King whom men thought was a-preparing for war was preparing for suffering, that He might bring peace, peace with God—for He reconciled us to God in His body on that tree; peace with ourselves—for now we may accept ourselves as God accepts us, free from guilt; and, peace with one another—for that death of His slew the enmity between man and man. Take up your palms and join the crowds, but wiser than the crowds and sing: "Hosanna! Blessed is He who comes in the name of the Lord!"

"Thus the disciples saw the Lord, and were glad."

(John 20:20b)

ΧΡΙΣΤΟΣ ΑΝΕΣΤΗ!

the king revealed

THE festival of Easter is the celebration of the
greatest event in human history. And yet, if
we had to describe how we feel about it, wouldn't
our description amount to this, that Easter is
something which has very little to do with us, that
somehow in this whole event we're not involved?
Aside from whatever sentimental significance the
day may have for us, most of us who celebrate
Easter regard it as the private victory of a private
individual. "Christ is risen," and bully for Him;
but as for us, we're not involved. Not that we're
bitter about it. Far from it. We're not bitter about
the proposition that two plus two make four.
That's a fact too, but it would still be a fact without us. It doesn't need you or me to prove it.

Jesus Christ is someone whom we love and admire, about whom we're very curious; we sympathize with Him every mournful step of the way, and we're terribly happy He rose from the dead, that the good won out in the end, but we can't see, particularly, that that has anything to do with us. Oh, of course, we believe that because He rose from the dead, some day the same thing will happen to us, but a man may still believe that and feel completely outside the whole event.

Easter to us is much like reading a page from another man's diary, a man who is our friend and whom we love. The record of his life, his thoughts, makes us laugh and cry. Whatever triumph he has inspires us, but after all it is *his* diary, *his* life, *his* triumph and not our own. Something of what he is or was may wash off on us, depending on our desire to imitate him, but there is nothing which links his life and destiny with our own. So Easter amounts to our merely getting a kind of vicarious glee in seeing what our children who watch television would call the "good guy licking the bad guy."

We talk of Easter as the proof that Jesus really was what He claimed to be, but again, the whole affair is more or less a case of our standing by and watching things take shape, just as a student in school watches a piece of litmus paper turn red or blue with acid or alkali without his having anything to do with it. At Easter we seem only to

be observers—what takes place in the arena between Christ and His enemies is His affair, not
ours—we're rooting for Him, we cheer when He
wins but, after all, His winning is a fact just like
any other fact. It didn't need you or me to happen.
We feel that Easter would be Easter without us;
that it would still be Easter if no one ever knew
about it. It has that objective, factual significance
about it which doesn't depend on you or me. We
are really not involved.

By all odds, the disciples of Jesus should have
felt the same way. They should have felt uninvolved in the whole affair. But they couldn't. And
the reason why they couldn't was that Jesus was
revealed *only to them*. It would have been most
convenient if there had been impartial eye-wit-
nesses to Jesus' resurrection, men who had no
"axe to grind" standing about the tomb and
watching the miracle take place. The disciples
could have been uninvolved then. The responsibility for making known that the One who was concealed in the form of a servant was really the
King wouldn't have been theirs at all then. They
would have needed only to take down the names
of the witnesses, as policemen do at the scene of
an accident, then to run off to Herod and Pilate
yelling: "There, you see? He rose from the dead!
And you don't need to go on our say-so. You can't
lay this thing to hallucinations or bias on our part.
We're out of it. We've got witnesses!" And you

and I would be out of it too. We'd merely need to cite the names of those ancient witnesses whenever the question came up, and then sit back and watch the doubter and the unbeliever squirm under the inexorable and incontrovertible truth of it.

But it wasn't that way for the disciples. They were the only ones who knew Christ had risen, because they were the only ones to whom He was revealed. We've got the catalogue of those disciple-witnesses in one of Paul's letters: first to Peter, then to the twelve, to five hundred, then to James and the other apostles, and last of all to Paul himself.

The Easter event was a fact, and all facts have that objective significance about them, that is, they remain facts no matter who doubts or believes them. But the peculiar situation in which the disciples found themselves was that the facts were made known to them alone! So they *could* be accused of having an "axe to grind"; they *could* be accused of hallucinations or prejudice. The Thing had taken place in such a way that men *could* bribe other men to say the disciples had come by night and stolen the body of Jesus away. They were not uninvolved. What happened at Easter depended on them. If anyone believed what happened then, it would only be because of them.

The long and short of it is that Easter is a fact and not a fiction only for believers. The evidence for the empty tomb is incontrovertible only for believers. There is no proof, anywhere, that Jesus rose from the dead but in the believer himself. So after all, we *are* involved! If Easter is an obvious fact to the world, then it is only because there are believers in the world. If it is nothing but a shabby, spring fiesta, it is because there are no believers in the world. For there is no demonstrable scientific proof anywhere that Jesus rose from the dead. We don't even know where He was buried. Right now in the city of Jerusalem, some Christians are huddling around one little hole in the ground and filling it with prayers and candles and incense, and others are huddling around another. Both are probably wrong. And we think we can celebrate the resurrection as though it were some obvious thing, taking place without us!

The simple fact is that Easter can't be celebrated without believers, for no one believes in Easter but a believer, and if there were no believers there would be no Easter. We can't stand by, assuming that this event has any meaning to the world, any meaning at all, without us. Easter can't be Easter without us. God isn't going to jump out of His heaven and write in the clouds, "Christ is risen!" He's planned it just this way, that the truth or the fiction of Easter depends on us.

If you live your life under the sign of God's

forgiving love, if your life is something strong and calm and beautiful, if there is that uncontrollable urge in your soul to love God, to serve His Christ by having pity on your neighbor, then, in time, someone will discover that He really rose from the dead. But if your life is a noisy, meaningless, useless thing, if you've lost your self-control and your love for the good and the true and the noble, all your songs and hymns and logical arguments for the existence of God and the resurrection are nonsense. You are a living, breathing denial of Easter. You're involved! To the degree your life reveals the light of that triumphant morning, to that degree—as far as the world is concerned—Christ is true and He arose.

If you suppose you are just an innocent bystander in this Easter event, then remember, if it were not for generations of passionately believing Christians, men and women who considered themselves most intimately involved, who spent their blood and their breath to keep the story of Easter alive, you wouldn't be able to enter a church door and take your seat and consider yourself just an innocent bystander!

Perhaps you remember that cracker-barrel philosopher, Jacques, in Shakespeare's *As You Like It*. He was the fellow who said, "All the world's a stage, And all the men and women merely players. . . . " He described the seven acts which make up the drama of a man's lifetime, from the babe "mewling and puking in the nurse's arms" to the last scene of all which ends this "strange eventful history: Second childishness and mere oblivion, Sans teeth, sans eyes, sans taste, sans everything." My interpretation may be all wrong, but I have always felt that Jacques was a kind of smug, supercilious fellow who poked fun at human existence as though he were a visitor from another planet, as though he weren't describing his own existence; as though he weren't involved. For the Christian at Easter, there is no question but what he is involved. To think otherwise is to play the fool, as Jacques did.

So the King who concealed His majesty and His dominion in the garments of a humble carpenter of Nazareth has revealed Himself for what He truly is—but only to the heart of the believer. True enough, He is King without us, He is God without us. And some day as the Bible says, He will be openly revealed to the whole world as the King. But in the little breath of human history between His going and His coming He is revealed only to His Church, to believers, and never apart from them. We are not uninvolved. Easter is not just the private victory of a private individual. Our destinies and our lives are linked with His, for the death He overcame was our own death, and not His; the battle in which He engaged was our battle, and not His own; and the victory He won was our victory, not His own.

When Elizabeth was crowned queen, we Americans were intensely interested. We've come to regard the English monarchy sympathetically, as a kind of symbol for everything the English hold dear. We sent representatives to march in their parade; a crowd of American diplomats and glamour girls were on hand to bow and curtsey to the queen. And yet, we were not involved. But for the English people, their sovereign's destiny is linked to their own. Though their kings and queens come to their thrones by right of accession, they would not be what they are if the people did not allow them to be. They would be sovereigns by blood right, but without a people, without the mass of humanity which holds them a sacred symbol of a brilliant history and an ancient tradition —of everything it holds dear—they would be only pretenders to the throne.

Without the believer Christ is King, the throne is His by divine right, but His Kingship and His throne are unrecognizable. Without the believer the Messiah, the Son of God, the Savior of the world who veiled Himself in the crucifixion and death of the Man Jesus, and rose fresh, strong and triumphant Easter morning, would still be hidden and unrevealed. It should make us tremble, tremble as the rocks in Arimathea's tomb, that whether or not the world believes it, whether or not men believe it, it is because of us! Whether or not the message of Easter is "Jesus Christ's body's still a-moulderin' in the grave" or "He is risen!" it is because of us. If He is the King, and if Easter is His royal coronation, His revelation, it is because of us. We are not uninvolved! Let Him be revealed, let Him put on His crown, let Him take His throne, here, in our hearts!